Collins

The Secret Life
of Dogs

David Taylor

First published in 2006 by Collins
an imprint of
HarperCollins Publishers
77–85 Fulham Palace Road
London W6 8JB

www.collins.co.uk

10 09 08 07
6 5 4 3 2 1

A catalogue record for this book is available from the British Library.

David Taylor asserts the moral right to be identified as the author of this work.

Editor: Heather Thomas
Designer: Rolando Ugolini
Photographer: Mark Read

ISBN-13: 978-0-00-724476-8
ISBN-10: 0-00-724476-2

Colour reproduction by Dot Gradations Ltd, UK
Printed and bound in Malaysia by Imago

What is dog
whispering?

A quiet word in one of those big ears, perhaps?
Well, not quite... but you've heard of Horse
Whispering and now we have Dog Whispering,
too. This utterly humane, psychological, almost
in some respects spiritual, approach to man-
dog relationships is based on a detailed study
of the dog's body language. Both you and your
dog need to develop an understanding of one
another's feelings and needs. You must act
in a way that is meaningful to your dog,
learning to communicate via body language
and without using your voice.

Do dogs sweat ?

This Westie is getting rather hot and bothered but is he sweating? Perhaps, but not to lose heat like humans do. The sweat glands in a dog's skin produce a secretion which, when broken down by bacteria, produces the typical 'doggy' smell. The glands in their paws help to keep the pads moist and supple for walking. Whereas we humans sweat when we're hot, our dogs get rid of unwanted calories by panting and losing heat through their sizeable tongues.

What's the point of **bottom-sniffing?**

Dogs do this all the time unlike us humans, who tend to regard it as unspeakably vulgar and over-familiar. So what's the point of sniffing other dogs' bottoms? Well, dogs possess glands just inside their anal orifice which produce a special secretion. They use this not only to leave proprietorial scent marks around their territory, but also to carry chemical messages, which are undecipherable by us but inform other dogs of the identity and sex of the bottom-owner.

Not quite the cat's
whiskers but...

Most dogs have whiskers although they are not usually as luxuriant as those of many cats. Their purpose, as tactile sensors, is to help the animal, when in darkness, to snuffle about for food or, if necessary, bury it. One wild species, the Bush Dog of South America, possesses especially luxurious whiskers – they probably have to search a lot harder for their next meal than this little pup!

How good is your
dog's memory?

We don't know much for certain about a dog's power of memory. Some experts believe that a dog will only remember things when there is some form of associated exterior 'trigger factor'. Without such a stimulus he doesn't think about past events. If you're away from your dog for over ten hours, they say, he will no longer pine for you. I doubt that many owners would agree!

A big yawn...
... or is it?

You and I yawn when we are tired or bored – or both. Our dogs also yawn, but not for the same reasons. With them it is a gesture that can be an indication of anxiety or uneasiness but, most frequently, it's a reassuring display on the part of a dominant dog addressing a lesser one which means 'Don't worry, I mean you no harm'.

Eyes that shine
in the dark

Although this little fellow hardly resembles the 'tiger burning bright in the forests of the night', dogs do see better in the dark than humans, although not as well as cats. Dogs' retinas contain far more rod cells – which are sensitive to low light – than ours do, and they also have a shining layer beneath them which reflects 'concentrated' light back through them.

This *tapetum lucidum* is not as well developed as in cats, so their eyes do not 'shine' in the dark to the same extent.

The power of
telepathy?

Are dogs telepathic? Well, many owners and even some scientists think so. It would explain how your pet knows that Dad's on his way home when his car is still a couple of miles away. Dogs can certainly distinguish the sound of familiar vehicles, but it isn't likely that, even with their powers of hearing, they can detect the family car so far away purely by using their ears.

Speed versus
stamina

The dog family has the stamina to be great marathon runners. African Wild Dog packs will chase their prey for hours over great distances and even kill lions when they are tiring. Among our domestic breeds the champion sprinters are Greyhounds, Salukis, Whippets, Afghan Hounds and Borzois. Racing Greyhounds and Salukis may approach an impressive 69kph (43mph), but this is slow compared to cheetahs who reach 129kph (80mph) over short distances.

How far and how
wide can dogs see?

The position of the eyes on a dog's head will determine his field of vision. Short-nosed breeds, like Pugs and Bulldogs, with eyes at the front of the head have overlapping fields of vision and thus better stereoscopic sight than long-nosed types with obliquely placed eyes and little overlap. This explains why long-nosed dogs, like Borzois and Salukis, often trip over obstacles when they are running at speed.

Round and round
before lying down

Dogs usually turn round and round in a tight circle before lying down. Why? This behaviour goes back to their ancestors – the wild dogs and wolves who were very much aware of the undesirability of bedding down on top of some irascible venomous snake or scorpion. Many of us humans do something similar, automatically, and without looking, brushing a seat with our hand before sitting down.

Barking up
the right tree

This dog appears to have something important to say. As well as using their body language, dogs communicate vocally. Each has his own individual voice with characteristics that come to be recognized by others of his kind. Dogs make different noises for a range of reasons: to announce their presence, to answer other dogs or stimulate them to vocalize, to indicate they are in defensive mode, to alert their family pack, or to warn off intruders on their territory.

Yes, yes, I know, but
you can't have one!

This little fellow has seen you eating a chocolate and is begging for one – don't do it! Chocolate contains a chemical, theobromine, which we humans can handle well but is toxic, even fatally so, if eaten by dogs. The small breeds are more susceptible than the large ones, and unsweetened dark chocolate is more dangerous than milk chocolate. So take some advice and don't ever give choccies to your pet!

You're as young as you feel

While some dogs continue to be alert and lively into ripe old age, most do not. Nowadays it is recognized that our canine friends can develop brain changes in old age that are like those found in human Alzheimer Disease patients. The symptoms are many and varied: confusion, increased sleeping, difficulty in recognizing familiar humans, forgetfulness, etc. As with elderly people, keeping your dog's body and mind active helps to ward off the condition.

How well can
your dog hear?

Dogs are excellent at hearing. They can detect noises well beyond the range of the human ear and can shut off their inner ear so as to filter out from the background din those sounds on which they wish to concentrate – they can handle cocktail parties really well! Such acute hearing also enables them to detect and give warning of imminent earthquakes and volcanic eruptions hours or even days before they occur.

When the dog bites...

The dog's principal weapon system is his teeth. His powerful jaw muscles enable him to clamp down with considerable power. A 20kg (44lb) mongrel has been found to exert a bite of 165kg (363lb) pressure, whereas the strongest of men, even under special training, can only manage a bite of 73kg (160lb).

Long live
our dogs...

It's a sad fact that big dogs don't live as long as the smaller breeds. Unfortunately, big means briefer. Few Wolfhounds like this one will reach 12 years of age, and Labrador Retrievers are seldom around to celebrate their fifteenth birthday. Some terriers, on the other hand, are still bouncing along at 20! The oldest dog on record was an Australian Cattle Dog that died in 1939 at just over 29 years old – trust an Aussie to knock up a big score!

Canine compasses
... or sat nav?

Dogs can sometimes find their way home over incredibly long distances. How do they do it? Well, they may be able to navigate by noting the position of the sun in combination with a biological clock which is situated somewhere within their bodies, and it is possible that, like birds, they have magnetic particles in their brains that act as compasses. Some scientists even surmise it may involve telepathy. Now what do you think? Is this dog lost or not?

He looks sharp
... he is sharp!

Animal psychologists consider the Border Collie to be the most intelligent of breeds. Other high IQ breeds are the Poodle, German Shepherd and Golden Retriever. At the thicker end of the scale are the Shih-Tzu, Basset Hound and, claimed to be the dimmest of all, the Afghan Hound. I beg to differ with the psychologists. I've known and treated some highly intelligent Afghans.

La dolce vita
... life is sweet

Unlike cats, dogs frequently have a sweet tooth.
In their mouths are taste receptors which are
linked to nerves. As with humans, these enable
them to respond to salty, bitter, acid and sweet
substances. Appreciating the sweet things in
life is unnecessary in highly carnivorous animals
such as cats, who lack this sweet receptor, but
dogs are more omnivorous, so they need to be
able to recognize them. I hear some Dalmatians
are particularly fond of Liquorice Allsorts.

Why is a dog's
nose wet?

To smell better – not as a health indicator for
the convenience of his owner! The nose is kept
moist by the secretions of special cells which
are stimulated by any new odours that happen
to be floating around in the air. These odours,
in the form of minute particles, dissolve in the
secretions and thus are brought into contact
with sensory cells that pass on information to
the dog's brain for analysis.

Big head...
big brain?

The human brain is much larger than that of
a dog. Even a big St. Bernard of similar weight
to a man has a brain which is about 15 per cent
of the weight of a human brain. While both
have sizeable chunks of brain involved in bodily
functions and movement, most of the canine
brain deals with the senses and recognition, and
very little is available for the formation of ideas.

One man
and his dog

The playful and loving relationship between man and his pet dog goes back many thousands of years. A 12,000-year-old grave in what is now Israel contains the skeleton of a man with one hand cradling a pup. When dogs died in Ancient Egypt they were often mummified and buried with their owners or in their own graves.

Is your dog
colour blind?

The retinas of our eyes and those of our dogs contain two types of light-sensitive cells - rods and cones. Rods are very sensitive, work well in low light levels but only appreciate black and white, whereas cones operate under good lighting conditions and can appreciate colour. Only five per cent of the dog's retinal cells are cones, so as a result dogs are colour blind, seeing only in black, white and shades of grey.

Communicating
from afar

Like their close relatives, the wolves, dogs often howl. Wolves do it to communicate with their fellow pack-members over long distances and as a bonding mechanism and, to some extent, it's the same with our pet dogs. Their howling is a form of communication with other dogs in the neighbourhood. Some breeds tend to be very noisy, especially terriers, Beagles, Collies, Norwegian Elkhounds, and the Finnish Spitz.

Can your dog
really count?

The answer is 'yes' – dogs can count, and they also have an understanding of addition and subtraction, which is very useful for pack-living, hunting animals like wolves from which they are descended. Experiments originally involving five-month-old babies have been applied to dogs with similar positive results. It seems that dogs, like many other mammals, may be able to count as high as seven.

If you don't use it
you'll lose it

Playing games with, and teaching tricks to
your dog keeps both of you fit, and also helps
to fend off the onset of senile changes in the
brain of your pet as it gets beyond about
eight years of age. Think up a variety of
different things for your dog to do every day,
encouraging him to use his grey matter. As
with you and me, so with the dog: 'If you
don't use it you'll lose it!'

The joys of
paddling pooches

Although the Bull Terrier has rather rudely stuck his tongue out at him, the well-mannered Retriever chooses to ignore the provocation! All three of these paddling pooches display very relaxed, non-aggressive body language, and aggro is not likely to break out on this occasion. Indeed, the facial expressions, tail positions and relaxed body postures of this trio all indicate that 'everything's cool, man!'

You *can* teach an
old dog new tricks

A dog is never too old to learn new tricks. 'Senior citizen' pets with stiff joints or failing sight can successfully be taught to raise a paw, 'to die for the queen' or to flip something balanced on their nose into the air and then catch it. Whatever the breed, size or shape of the dog it can learn to do something, and crossbreeds are frequently better at thinking for themselves than even Border Collies!

What do we mean by canine intelligence ?

There are three separate forms: learning ability and problem solving; the ability to respond appropriately to commands; and breed-related instinctive intelligence. Comparing breed intelligence is difficult. How to compare breeds that have been developed as specialists: terriers adept at working below ground; collies, the expert sheep herders; or the Borzoi, a keen-sighted, speedy hunter? And what about the good old mongrel, so often highly quick-witted?

How sensitive
is a dog's nose?

Depending upon the breed, our dogs' noses are 10,000 to 100,000 times more sensitive than ours, and their brains have 40 times more nerve cells involved in scent recognition than we do. Just imagine! This would enable them to pick out one rotten apple in 2 billion barrels! So it's no wonder that they are brilliant at sniffing out explosives, drugs, folk buried under rubble, exquisite truffles, and even certain tumours and other diseases in human patients.

Dogs 'talk'
with their tails

Yes, it really is true – dogs can talk to us and each other with their tails. For example; a broad tail wag means: 'I like you'. A slight tail wag means: 'I see you're looking at me. You like me, don't you?' A tail held up and curved forwards over the back says: 'I'm top dog!' And a tail held down near the hind legs with legs bent slightly inwards is declaring: 'I feel a bit insecure'.

Doggie paddle

Dogs are natural swimmers though they eschew the crawl and breast stroke and only ever use the dog paddle! Some are champions in the water. Jake, a Golden Retriever, swam from the prison island of Alcatraz to San Francisco in 42 minutes in August 2005. The only non-human entrant among 500 swimmers in a competition, he came seventy-second! He was the first dog ever recorded to have made the crossing.

Do dogs smile?
Yes, of course!

The canine smile is very similar to the typical aggressive snarl with lips pulled back, but almost always with less baring of teeth and certainly not the canine (fang) teeth. While you and I may smile when amused or happy, dogs, though undoubtedly showing an appreciation of humorous situations, only smile when pleased.

David Taylor

David Taylor is a highly respected veterinary surgeon. The founder of the International Zoo Veterinary Group, he travels the world treating a wide range of animals. He is the author of many petcare books and has presented and featured in several TV shows.

Acknowledgements

The publishers would like to thank the following for kindly allowing us to feature their dogs: A-Z Animals and Tara, Louise Dyer and Alfie, Jinnie Chalton Ena and Tosca, Jacqui Hurst and Digby, Bryony James and Barney, Emma Johnson and Bella, Michael Ruggins and Max, Alex Smith and Jess, Fiona Worthingon and Pepper. Our thanks also to the staff and dogs of the Mayhew Animal Home (www.mayhewanimalhome.org, 0208 969 0178) and to Pet Planet (www.petplanet.co.uk tel: 0845 345 0723) for supplying props for photography.